SPOTLIGHT ON WEATHER AND NATURAL DISASTERS

STORMS, FLOODS, AND EROSION

SARAH MACHAJEWSKI

PowerKiDS
press™

NEW YORK

Published in 2019 by The Rosen Publishing Group, Inc.
29 East 21st Street, New York, NY 10010

Editor: Hannah Fields
Cover Design: Michael Flynn
Interior Layout: Tanya Dellaccio

Photo Credits: Cover (background) Cammie Czuchnicki/Shutterstock.com; cover Kim Westerskov/Photographer's Choice/Getty Images; p. 5 Boyd Hendrikse/Shutterstock.com; p. 7 (diagram) Spencer Sutton/Science Source/Getty Images; p. 7 (igneous rock) vvoe/Shutterstock.com; p. 7 (sedimentary rock) Kashin/Shutterstock.com; p. 7 (metamorphic rock) www.sandatlas.org/Shutterstock.com; p. 8 (Himalayas) Volodymyr Goinyk/Shutterstock.com; p. 8 (rock structure) Konoplytska/Shutterstock.com; p. 9 https://commons.wikimedia.org/wiki/File:Spelterini_Matterhorn_1910.jpg; p. 10 Maridav/Shutterstock.com; p. 11 Daniela Constantinescu/Shutterstock.com; p. 12 Lawoowoo/Shutterstock.com; p. 13 Vizual Studio/Shutterstock.com; p. 14 Courtesy of National Oceanic & Atmospheric Adminstration; p. 15 Martin Haas/Shutterstock.com; p. 17 Carol Blaker/Shutterstock.com; pp. 18, 19 Scott Olson/Getty Images News/Getty Images; p. 21 YASUYOSHI CHIBA/AFP/Getty Images; p. 22 Edson Vandeira/National Geographic/Getty Images.

Library of Congress Cataloging-in-Publication Data

Names: Machajewski, Sarah, author.
Title: Storms, floods, and erosion / Sarah Machajewski.
Description: New York : PowerKids Press, [2019] | Series: Spotlight on weather and natural disasters | Includes bibliographical references and index.
Identifiers: LCCN 2017059692| ISBN 9781508169116 (library bound) | ISBN
   9781508169130 (pbk.) | ISBN 9781508169147 (6 pack)
Subjects: LCSH: Weather--Juvenile literature. | Catastrophes
   (Geology)--Juvenile literature. | Historical geology--Juvenile literature.
Classification: LCC QC981.3 .M265 2018 | DDC 551.6--dc23
LC record available at https://lccn.loc.gov/2017059692

Manufactured in the United States of America

CPSIA Compliance Information: Batch #CS18PK For further information contact Rosen Publishing, New York, New York at 1-800-237-9932.

CONTENTS

CHAPTER ONE

A CONSTANTLY CHANGING PLANET

Planet Earth is billions of years old. Long ago, when the planet formed, it looked very different from what we see today. Huge rocks, steep cliffs, islands, lowlands—Earth's landscapes have been shaped, shifted, created, and destroyed over time. Some of these changes have occurred over billions of years—and the process continues even as you're reading. Some changes happen in an instant, and their impact is much more **dramatic**. In recent years especially, **extreme** weather events have **devastated** areas all over the globe, affecting not just the landscapes, but the people who call them home, too.

Whether through **erosion**, storms, floods, or extreme weather, Earth's landscapes are always changing. Let's look at some of the planet's unbelievable forces of nature and their impact.

These rock formations were shaped over time by nature's powerful forces.

CHAPTER TWO

THE ROCK CYCLE

Many of Earth's rocks are as old as the planet itself. In fact, our planet is made of layers of rocks that constantly change, form, and break down. This process is called the rock cycle. The rock cycle traces how rocks form deep inside the earth, travel to the surface, wear away, and often sink back into the ground.

Metamorphic rocks are those that form in the heat and pressure deep underground. **Volcanic** explosions send these rocks and magma, or partly liquid, hot rock, to the earth's surface. At the surface, magma is called lava. As the lava cools and hardens, it becomes igneous rocks. Erosion can break rocks into tiny bits called sediment, which water carries to lower ground, often the bottom of a body of water. As layers of sediment build up, time and pressure turn it into sedimentary rocks. Forces deep inside Earth will cause these rocks to shift, pushing them to the surface or deeper into the ground, and the rock cycle starts all over again.

WEATHERING

TRANSPORT

MELTING

METAMORPHISM

SEDIMENT

MAGMA

IGNEOUS
ROCK

METAMORPHIC
ROCK

SEDIMENTARY
ROCK

Rocks are constantly changing.
The rock cycle shows us how!

CHAPTER THREE

EXTREME EROSION

Many rocks are constantly exposed to the natural elements. None are safe from the effects of erosion. Erosion created the high peaks in the Himalayas of Nepal, the beautiful sandstone arches in Utah in the United States, and the sharp curve of the Matterhorn on the border of Switzerland and Italy.

HIMALAYAS, NEPAL

SANDSTONE ARCHES, UTAH

Wind erosion is powerful. Even light winds are powerful enough to move tiny grains of rock and soil from one area to another. Strong winds can carry enough dust to create blinding dust storms! In 2004, strong winds carried 45 million tons (40.8 mt) of dust from Africa to Brazil.

Water erodes landscapes, too. As waves crash against rocks, the rocks wear away into tiny grains of sand. Water's powerful force creates cliffs and caves. It even created the Grand Canyon. Water erosion can greatly affect people's lives. Many people choose to live and build along beaches and coastlines. As the land disappears, structures can fall and people can lose their homes.

Water can erode land even when the water is frozen. Glaciers, or huge masses of ice, can be responsible for erosion. Glaciers are very heavy, and they can sit on top of land. As they move, they pick up tiny bits of soil and rock in their path and carry them to other places.

Glaciers are so heavy that they carve and shape the rocks below them. Over hundreds and thousands of years, glaciers have created stunning landforms such as cirques (bowl-shaped landforms), arêtes (jagged, narrow ridges), and horns (steep peaks).

When glaciers retreat, they leave many interesting clues. Glacial lakes form when a glacier leaves a hole behind and then melts, filling the hole with water. Glaciers have carried boulders and deposited them in **foreign** places. That's how powerful they are!

This glacier looks like a river of ice. As the ice advances and retreats, it may carve valleys and other interesting landforms in the rocks below.

CHAPTER FOUR

SUPER-DESTRUCTIVE STORMS

Whipping winds, pounding rain, driving snow–these extreme forms of weather can be powerful and destructive. Each of these can form strong storms, or **disturbances** of the **atmosphere**. Storms bring **precipitation**, strong winds, and often lightning and thunder.

Even storms that seem minor can cause a lot of damage. They may knock over many trees.

You may have experienced thunderstorms where you live. Many areas also experience hurricanes, tornadoes, or blizzards. A hurricane is a large, rotating storm, called a tropical cyclone, that forms over a warm ocean. Hurricanes have very strong winds. A tornado is a strong, spinning funnel of air. A blizzard is a snowstorm or blowing snow with strong winds. These storms can cause a lot of damage when they hit. They can even claim lives.

CHAPTER FIVE

TERRIBLE TORNADO

Tornadoes can be easily recognized by their tall funnel of moving air. Tornadoes often form in thunderstorms when winds quickly change speed and direction. The storm's rising air tips the swirling winds to a vertical position.

Tornado funnels have been measured at more than 600 feet (182.9 m) wide, and their winds can move up to

Tornadoes might be unstoppable, but the more scientists learn about them, the more they can do to keep people safe.

250 miles (402.3 km) per hour. Tornadoes can move fast, but they don't usually last long.

Tornadoes are very dangerous because the strong winds can destroy everything in their path. They can lift all kinds of objects, including cars, homes, and trees, into the air. In 2011, one of the strongest tornadoes ever recorded in the United States hit Joplin, Missouri. The tornado cloud was measured at nearly 1 mile (1.6 km) wide, with winds that measured up to 200 miles (321.9 km) per hour.

CHAPTER SIX

HURRICANES AND FLOODS

Hurricanes are dangerous storms that shouldn't be taken lightly. Hurricanes are marked by strong winds, lots of rain, and thunder. They form over oceans in spots where warm, moist air rises and forms a growing system of clouds and wind.

When a hurricane makes its way to land, watch out! The strong winds can destroy homes, rip out trees, and **hurl** heavy objects through the air. The rain can be destructive too, causing landslides and major flooding.

Floods occur after heavy rainfall, when there is more water than the ground and waterways can hold. Areas that are usually dry become covered in water. Flash floods are periods of rapid flooding. They're the most dangerous type of flood because they happen quickly and they're unpredictable. They can occur in an instant, without warning.

Hurricanes create waves that slam into coastal areas. These waves can damage or destroy structures and harm people.

CHAPTER SEVEN

FLOODS HIT TEXAS

Hurricanes tend to hit states in the southern and southeastern United States. These states are located near where tropical cyclones often form and move. In August 2017, Hurricane Harvey hit Texas and caused major flooding. Parts of the state sat underwater for several days.

The hurricane dropped about 50 inches (127 cm) of rain on Houston, Texas, alone. Thousands of people

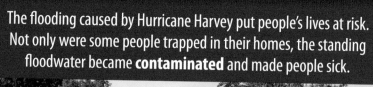
The flooding caused by Hurricane Harvey put people's lives at risk. Not only were some people trapped in their homes, the standing floodwater became **contaminated** and made people sick.

were forced to leave their homes as floodwaters began to rise. In parts of Houston, people's homes and cars filled with water, trapping people and their pets. A number of people died.

Some scientists say flooding caused by Harvey actually warped Earth's crust. The floodwaters were so heavy that they caused the crust to sink by about 0.8 inches (2 cm). Scientists think the crust will return to its original height over time.

CHAPTER EIGHT

TSUNAMIS

Dramatic weather events and their impacts are often easy to see. However, sometimes the cause isn't as easy to see because it happens deep in the ocean. Tsunamis are a series of ocean waves caused by disruptions in the ocean. These disruptions may be the eruption of an undersea volcano, an earthquake under the seafloor, or a landslide. Most tsunamis are caused by earthquakes.

Tsunamis are considered natural **disasters**. The most dangerous tsunamis are those caused by earthquakes close to coastlines. Communities that are on the shore and built close to sea level are most at risk.

When a tsunami occurs, huge waves of water can hit the land. The force of this water can destroy homes and cities and alter landscapes in the blink of an eye. Flooding can affect the area for days after the original waves.

In 2011, Japan was hit by a tsunami caused by an earthquake. The earthquake was so strong that it could be felt even in Antarctica. The tsunami flooded 217 square miles (562 sq km) of land and almost 16,000 people died. This picture shows what part of Japan looked like after the event.

CHAPTER NINE

STUDY AND PREPARE!

All areas of the planet are likely to experience extreme weather at some point. The land changes through storms, flooding, and erosion. These powerful forces are always at work, altering Earth's landscape before our eyes—both in an instant and over thousands of years.

While these weather events can be fun to study, they are very dangerous to witness. Storms, flooding, and erosion affect people all over the world. People must adapt to the conditions and sometimes even leave their homes to find safety. Scientists continue to study these natural events so that we can understand them better. We need to better understand the science at work behind storms, flooding, and erosion and be better prepared to deal with them in the future.

GLOSSARY

atmosphere (AT-muh-sfeer) The mixture of gases that surround a planet.

contaminated (kuhn-TAA-muh-nay-tuhd) Polluted.

devastate (DEH-vuh-stayt) To destroy much or most of something or to cause emotional suffering.

disaster (dih-ZAS-tuhr) Something that happens suddenly and causes much suffering and loss for many people.

disturbance (dih-STUHR-bunts) A breakdown of peaceful and law-abiding behavior.

dramatic (druh-MAH-tik) Sudden and striking.

erosion (ih-ROH-zuhn) The wearing away of the earth's surface by wind, water, or ice.

extreme (ik-STREEM) Very great in degree.

foreign (FOR-uhn) Not native to an area.

hurl (HUHRL) To throw with great force.

precipitation (prih-sih-puh-TAY-shuhn) Water that falls to the ground as hail, mist, rain, sleet, or snow.

volcanic (vahl-KAN-nick) Having to do with a volcano, or an opening in a planet's surface through which hot, liquid rock sometimes flows.

INDEX

PRIMARY SOURCE LIST

Page 9
Spelterini Matterhorn. Photograph. Taken by Eduard Spelterini. 1910. From Wikimedia Commons.

Page 14
Tornado in mature stage. Photograph. Taken by D. Burgess. April 10, 1979. NOAA's National Severe Storms Laboratory (NSSL) Collection.

Page 18
Flooding in Houston after Hurricane Harvey. Photograph. Taken by Scott Olson. August 31, 2017. Getty Images News.

Page 19
Flooding in Houston after Hurricane Harvey. Photograph. Taken by Scott Olson. September 3, 2017. Getty Images News.

WEBSITES